Table of Content

Chapter 1: Understanding the Importance of Difficult Dialogue

The Impact of Avoiding Tough Conversations

Tough conversations with employees are an inevitable part of management. These discussions can cover a range of topics, such as addressing performance issues, discussing disciplinary actions, or managing conflicts. Although these conversations may be uncomfortable and challenging, avoiding them can have severe consequences for both the employer and the employees involved.

One of the most significant impacts of avoiding tough conversations is the deterioration of trust within the workplace. Employees rely on their employers to provide guidance, support, and constructive feedback. When tough conversations are avoided, employees may feel neglected and undervalued. This can lead to a decline in morale, employee disengagement, and an overall decrease in productivity. Without clear communication and open dialogue, employees may struggle to understand expectations, resulting in confusion and frustration.

Furthermore, avoiding tough conversations can create a toxic work environment. Unresolved issues can fester and escalate, leading to increased tension and conflict among employees. This can disrupt team dynamics and hinder collaboration. Ultimately, it may result in a high turnover rate as employees seek a healthier work environment elsewhere.

Additionally, avoiding tough conversations can hinder professional growth and development. Constructive feedback plays a crucial role in helping employees identify areas for improvement and develop their skills. By avoiding these conversations, employers deny employees the opportunity to learn, grow, and reach their full potential. This stagnation can be detrimental to both the individual and the organization's progress.

On the other hand, embracing tough conversations can have positive outcomes. When approached with empathy, respect, and clear communication, these discussions can foster trust, strengthen relationships, and drive positive change. They provide an opportunity to address underlying issues, resolve conflicts, and promote a culture of continuous improvement. By engaging in tough conversations, employers demonstrate their commitment to their employees' growth and well-being.

To navigate tough conversations effectively, employers must be prepared, listen actively, and provide constructive feedback. They should approach these discussions with a growth mindset, focusing on finding solutions rather than assigning blame. Additionally, creating a safe and supportive environment where employees feel comfortable sharing their concerns is crucial.

To sum up, it may seem easier to avoid tough conversations, but the long-term consequences can be detrimental. Employers must acknowledge the importance of addressing difficult topics head-on. The impact of avoiding these conversations can lead to a decline in trust, a toxic work environment, and obstacles to professional growth. By embracing these conversations, employers can create a culture of open dialogue, mutual respect, and continuous improvement.

Recognizing the Benefits of Addressing Issues Head-On

In the fast-paced and competitive world of business, employers often find themselves faced with the challenging task of addressing difficult conversations with their employees. These conversations can range from discussing performance issues, conflicts among team members, or even sensitive personal matters. However, it is essential for employers to recognize the benefits of addressing these issues head-on rather than avoiding them.

One of the key benefits of addressing issues head-on is the potential for resolving the problem at its early stages. By recognizing and addressing the problem promptly, employers can prevent it from escalating into a more significant issue that could potentially disrupt the entire workplace. Early intervention allows employers to provide necessary support, guidance, and resources to help employees overcome challenges and improve their performance.

Addressing issues head-on also promotes transparency and trust within the organization. Employees appreciate open and honest communication from their employers, even when discussing difficult topics. By initiating tough conversations, employers demonstrate their commitment to creating a supportive and fair work environment. This fosters a culture of trust, where employees feel comfortable expressing their concerns, seeking help, and providing feedback.

Furthermore, addressing issues head-on allows employers to identify and rectify underlying problems that may be affecting employee morale and productivity. By engaging in open dialogue, employers can gain valuable insights into the root causes of issues and implement necessary changes to prevent similar problems from arising in the future. This proactive approach to problem-solving can lead to improved employee satisfaction, increased motivation, and enhanced overall performance.

It is crucial for employers to recognize that ignoring or avoiding tough conversations can have detrimental effects on both the individual employee and the entire organization. Unresolved issues can lead to decreased productivity, increased absenteeism, and even a toxic work environment. By stepping up and addressing these issues head-on, employers can create a positive and supportive work environment that encourages growth, development, and collaboration.

It is important for employers to recognize the advantages of confronting issues directly when dealing with difficult conversations with employees. By taking prompt action to address problems, promoting transparency and trust, and resolving underlying issues, employers can establish a healthy work environment that encourages employee growth and productivity. Although difficult conversations can be challenging, the long-term benefits far outweigh the temporary discomfort of addressing them head-on.

Common Challenges Employers Face in Difficult Conversations

Difficult conversations with employees are an inevitable part of being an employer. Whether it's addressing performance issues, discussing sensitive topics, or providing feedback, these conversations can be challenging for various reasons. Understanding and overcoming the common challenges that employers face in difficult conversations is crucial to fostering a positive work environment and achieving productive outcomes.

One of the primary challenges employers encounter is fear of confrontation. Many employers avoid difficult conversations due to the fear of conflict or potential negative reactions from employees. However, avoiding these conversations only exacerbates the problem, leading to decreased employee morale and productivity. Overcoming this challenge requires developing effective communication skills, including active listening, empathy, and assertiveness. By approaching these conversations with a focus on problem-solving rather than confrontation, employers can create a more open and collaborative environment.

Another challenge is the lack of preparation. Difficult conversations require careful planning and preparation to ensure that the message is delivered effectively. Employers often struggle with finding the right words or understanding how to navigate sensitive topics. To overcome this challenge, employers should invest time in preparing for the conversation, including gathering relevant information, practicing their delivery, and anticipating potential reactions. By being well-prepared, employers can convey their message clearly and confidently, increasing the chances of a successful outcome.

Emotional reactions from employees can also pose a significant challenge. Difficult conversations may trigger strong emotions, such as anger, defensiveness, or sadness, which can hinder effective communication. Employers need to be prepared for these emotional reactions and approach them with empathy and understanding. Creating a safe space for employees to express their emotions and actively listening to their concerns can help alleviate tension and foster a more constructive dialogue.

Finally, a lack of follow-up and accountability is a common challenge faced by employers. Difficult conversations often require follow-up actions or changes in behavior. However, without proper accountability measures, these conversations can remain ineffective. Employers should establish clear expectations, set realistic goals, and provide ongoing support to employees. Regular check-ins and feedback sessions can help ensure that the conversation's outcomes are implemented and progress is made.

In summary, talking to employees about tough topics is something every boss has to do. When bosses recognize and deal with the typical issues that come up in these talks, they can learn how to handle them well. Getting over the fear of confrontation, getting ready ahead of time, handling emotions, and making sure everyone takes responsibility are crucial for creating a good work atmosphere and having successful talks about hard stuff.

Chapter 2: Preparing for Difficult Conversations

Assessing the Situation and Identifying the Need for a Conversation

In the world of supervising staff, tough talks are bound to happen. Whether it's dealing with performance problems, conflicts, or touchy subjects, bosses frequently have to have challenging discussions with their team. But before jumping into these hard talks, it's important to evaluate the situation and recognize the necessity for a conversation.

Assessing the situation involves taking a step back to evaluate the current state of affairs. Is there an ongoing problem that needs to be addressed? Are there any patterns of behavior that are affecting team dynamics or overall productivity? Assessing the situation requires a thorough understanding of the issue at hand, as well as its impact on both the individual employee and the broader organization.

Identifying the need for a conversation is equally important. Sometimes, employers may be tempted to avoid difficult discussions due to fear of confrontation or a desire to maintain harmony. However, sweeping issues under the rug only allows them to fester and potentially escalate into more significant problems. By recognizing the need for a conversation, employers can proactively address concerns and work towards finding a resolution.

One way to identify the need for a conversation is by observing changes in employee behavior. Is someone consistently underperforming or displaying a negative attitude? Are there signs of disengagement or a decline in motivation? These indicators can serve as red flags, signaling the need for a conversation. Additionally, feedback from other team members or complaints from customers or clients can highlight areas that require attention.

Furthermore, employers should consider the impact of unresolved issues on team morale and overall performance. A toxic work environment can have detrimental effects on employee engagement, productivity, and even retention. Recognizing the need for a conversation can help employers address these issues before they escalate and create a negative work culture.

To sum up, it's essential to assess the situation and recognize when a conversation is needed when dealing with tough discussions with employees. By doing so, employers can handle concerns early, enhance team dynamics, and promote a positive work environment. Though difficult, addressing these conversations directly helps manage employees effectively and create a more productive and harmonious workplace.

Setting Clear Objectives and Desired Outcomes

In any workplace, there are bound to be difficult conversations that employers must navigate with their employees. These conversations can arise due to performance issues, conflicts, or even disciplinary actions. However, handling these tough conversations effectively is essential for maintaining a healthy working environment and fostering positive employee relationships.

One crucial step in managing tough conversations with employees is setting clear objectives and desired outcomes. By establishing these goals from the outset, employers can ensure that the conversation remains focused and productive. This subchapter will explore the importance of setting clear objectives and desired outcomes, providing practical strategies for employers to implement.

Clear objectives serve as a roadmap for the conversation, enabling employers to communicate their concerns or expectations effectively. By clearly defining the purpose of the conversation, employers can minimize misunderstandings and ensure that both parties are on the same page. Additionally, setting objectives helps employers stay on track during the discussion, preventing any unnecessary digressions that could hinder the resolution process.

Desired outcomes, on the other hand, provide a vision of the ideal result of the conversation. Employers should identify what they hope to achieve through the dialogue, whether it is improved performance, conflict resolution, or a change in behavior. Clearly articulating these outcomes helps employers communicate their expectations to employees and provides a shared goal to work towards.

To set clear objectives and desired outcomes, employers can follow a few key strategies. Firstly, it is important to conduct thorough preparation before the conversation. Employers should gather all relevant information, identify specific concerns, and formulate desired outcomes. This preparation will allow employers to approach the conversation with confidence and clarity.

During the conversation, employers should clearly communicate their objectives and desired outcomes to the employee. They should explain the purpose of the conversation and listen to the employee's perspective to foster open communication. By involving the employee in the goal-setting process, employers can increase their commitment to achieving the desired outcomes.

Lastly, employers should ensure that the objectives and desired outcomes are measurable and realistic. Setting specific targets and timelines allows employers to track progress and hold employees accountable. Realistic goals also help prevent frustration and demotivation, ensuring that both parties are committed to working towards a feasible outcome.

To conclude, having clear objectives and desired outcomes is essential when dealing with tough conversations with employees. By setting these goals, employers can keep the conversation focused, enhance employee engagement and work towards mutually beneficial resolutions. By following the strategies outlined in this subsection, employers can effectively handle difficult conversations and cultivate a positive and productive work environment.

Gathering Relevant Information and Documentation

When dealing with difficult conversations with employees, it's essential to gather the right information and documentation. As an employer, it's your duty to have all the facts and evidence before having any tough discussions. This section will help you through the process of gathering information and documentation, so you can approach these conversations with confidence and fairness.

The first step in gathering information is to clearly define the purpose of the conversation. Whether it's addressing performance issues, misconduct, or any other sensitive matter, having a clear objective will enable you to focus your efforts on collecting the right information. Identify what kind of documentation, records, or evidence will be essential in supporting your claims or concerns.

Next, it is important to consult any existing policies, procedures, or employment contracts that might be relevant to the situation at hand. Familiarize yourself with these documents to ensure that you are adhering to the guidelines and processes laid out by your organization. These documents can also serve as a reference point during the conversation, providing a clear framework for discussing any shortcomings or violations.

In addition to reviewing internal documents, it may be necessary to gather external information. This can include reviewing any relevant industry regulations, laws, or guidelines that may impact the situation. Stay up to date with any legal requirements or best practices to ensure that your conversation is both legally sound and ethical.

When it comes to gathering evidence, it is crucial to maintain confidentiality and respect the privacy of all parties involved. Collect any documentation, such as emails, performance reviews, or witness statements, that can provide objective evidence of the issues at hand. However, be mindful of any sensitive or personal information, ensuring that it is handled with the utmost care and discretion.

Lastly, organizing the information and documentation in a clear and logical manner will greatly assist you during the conversation. Create a comprehensive file that includes all relevant documents, making it easier for you to refer to specific points or evidence when necessary. This will also demonstrate your professionalism and preparedness, enhancing your credibility as an employer.

Lastly, gathering relevant information and documentation is a critical step in navigating tough conversations with employees. By taking the time to gather the necessary facts and evidence, consulting internal and external resources, and organizing the information effectively, you will be well-equipped to conduct these conversations with fairness, clarity, and confidence.

Chapter 3: Creating a Positive and Supportive Environment

Establishing Trust and Open Communication

In the contemporary dynamic work landscape, employers frequently encounter demanding discussions with their staff. These challenging dialogues encompass a spectrum of issues, from tackling performance concerns to delving into sensitive subjects like grievances or conflicts. Nevertheless, adeptly managing these intricate conversations is essential for cultivating a thriving and efficient work atmosphere. To attain this objective, employers need to prioritize the establishment of trust and open lines of communication with their team members.

Trust is the foundation of any successful working relationship. It is essential for both parties to feel comfortable and secure in sharing their thoughts, concerns, and ideas. Building trust begins with creating a safe space where employees feel respected and valued. Employers can achieve this by actively listening to their employees, providing constructive feedback, and maintaining confidentiality when required.

Open communication is equally vital in handling tough conversations with employees. Employers must encourage an environment where employees feel confident in expressing their opinions and discussing any challenges they may be facing. By fostering a culture of open communication, employers empower their employees to voice their concerns, seek guidance, and collaborate effectively.

To establish trust and open communication, employers can implement a few strategies. First, it is crucial to set clear expectations and goals from the start. This ensures that employees understand what is expected of them and how their performance will be evaluated. Regular check-ins and performance reviews can also provide a platform for open dialogue and feedback.

Moreover, employers should encourage a two-way communication approach, where employees are encouraged to provide input, ask questions, and contribute to decision-making processes. This fosters a sense of ownership and involvement, making employees feel valued and respected.

In difficult conversations, empathy plays a significant role. Employers must strive to understand their employees' perspectives and emotions, acknowledging their feelings and concerns. This empathy helps create a safe environment where employees feel heard and supported.

Lastly, employers should be transparent in their communication. Communicating openly about the organization's goals, challenges, and changes helps build trust and credibility. Employees appreciate honesty, even if the news is not always positive. Transparent communication fosters a sense of inclusion and ensures that employees are well-informed.

To sum up, establishing trust and open communication is crucial for navigating tough conversations with employees. By creating a safe and respectful environment, setting clear expectations, encouraging open dialogue, and practicing empathy and transparency, employers can foster a culture of trust and open communication. This, in turn, leads to stronger working relationships, increased employee engagement, and a more productive work environment.

Active Listening and Empathy

When engaging in challenging discussions with employees, possessing active listening skills coupled with empathy stands out as a crucial asset for employers. The adept application of these two qualities can significantly amplify comprehension, foster trust, and ultimately result in more fruitful conversations.

Active listening goes beyond simply hearing what the employee is saying. It involves fully engaging with the speaker, giving them your undivided attention, and making a conscious effort to

understand their perspective. By actively listening, employers can gain valuable insights into their employees' thoughts, feelings, and concerns, which can help in addressing any issues more effectively.

To practice active listening, it is crucial to give the employee ample space to express themselves without interruption. Avoid jumping to conclusions or making assumptions, as this can hinder the open flow of communication. Instead, ask clarifying questions to ensure you have a clear understanding of their point of view. Paraphrasing their statements can also be a useful technique, as it demonstrates that you are actively listening and encourages the employee to elaborate further.

Empathy, on the other hand, involves putting yourself in the employee's shoes and genuinely understanding their emotions and experiences. It requires recognizing and acknowledging their feelings, even if you may not agree with them. By showing empathy, employers create a safe and supportive space for employees to express themselves, which can foster trust and encourage open dialogue.

To cultivate empathy, it is essential to demonstrate compassion and understanding. Acknowledge the employee's emotions and validate their experiences, even if you do not share the same perspective. Avoid dismissing or trivializing their concerns, as this can undermine the trust and rapport you are trying to build. Instead, offer support and reassurance, letting them know that you genuinely care about their well-being.

By combining active listening and empathy, employers can create an environment where tough conversations with employees become opportunities for growth and understanding. These skills enable employers to truly hear and understand their employees' perspectives, which can lead to more effective problem-solving and conflict resolution.

Remember, active listening and empathy are not innate abilities but skills that can be developed and honed over time. With practice, employers can master these qualities and navigate tough conversations with employees in a way that fosters positive relationships and promotes a healthy work environment.

Managing Emotions and Remaining Calm

Navigating challenging discussions with employees requires employers to master the vital skill of managing their own emotions and maintaining composure. These conversations frequently carry emotional weight, characterized by tension and anxiety. Nevertheless, it is imperative for employers to remain poised and level-headed, ensuring effective communication and successful resolution.

Emotions can run high during tough conversations, both for the employer and the employee. As an employer, it is imperative to recognize and acknowledge your own emotions before engaging in these discussions. Take a moment to reflect on how you are feeling and what may be triggering those emotions. By doing so, you can better understand your own biases and prevent them from influencing the conversation.

Remaining calm during difficult conversations is not about suppressing emotions but rather understanding and managing them. Emotions can provide valuable insights into the underlying concerns and issues at hand. However, it is crucial to express these emotions in a constructive and controlled manner. Remember, maintaining a calm demeanor sets a positive tone for the conversation and encourages open dialogue.

One effective strategy for managing emotions is to practice active listening. By actively listening, you show empathy and understanding towards the employee, which can help defuse tension. Pay close attention to their words, tone, and body language. This will not only help you understand their perspective better but also demonstrate your commitment to resolving the issue.

Another helpful technique is to take regular breaks during the conversation. If you notice emotions escalating, suggest a short pause to collect thoughts and regain composure. This break can give both parties an opportunity to reflect on the discussion and approach it with a renewed sense of calm.

Lastly, it is crucial to separate the person from the problem. When engaging in tough conversations, focus on the issue at hand rather than attacking the individual. Keep the conversation solution-oriented, focusing on finding common ground and mutually beneficial outcomes.

To conclude, managing emotions and remaining calm during difficult conversations with employees is a vital skill for employers. By recognizing and acknowledging your own emotions, practicing active listening, taking breaks, and focusing on the problem rather than the person, you can foster a more positive and productive dialogue. Remember, maintaining composure sets the stage for effective communication and resolution, ultimately strengthening your relationship with your employees and driving organizational success.

Chapter 4: Effective Communication Strategies

Using Clear and Concise Language

In any workplace, difficult conversations with employees are inevitable. These conversations may involve addressing poor performance, addressing misconduct, providing negative feedback, or discussing sensitive topics. As an employer, it is crucial to navigate these conversations effectively and with empathy. One way to achieve this is by using clear and concise language.

Clear and concise language is vital in tough conversations with employees as it helps to eliminate misunderstandings and misinterpretations. When you communicate clearly, you ensure that your message is understood as intended, reducing the chances of confusion or ambiguity. This is particularly important when discussing sensitive or challenging subjects, as even a slight miscommunication can lead to increased tension or even legal issues.

To use clear and concise language, start by being prepared. Before engaging in a difficult conversation, take the time to gather all the necessary information and organize your thoughts. Clearly define the purpose of the conversation, identify the key points you need to address, and consider the employee's perspective. This preparation will help you communicate your message effectively and confidently.

During the conversation, strive to be concise and avoid unnecessary jargon or technical terms. Use simple and straightforward language that is easily understandable. Break down complex concepts into smaller, digestible parts, and provide examples or analogies to help illustrate your points. This approach will ensure that your message resonates with the employee and reduces the chances of confusion.

Additionally, utilize active listening skills to confirm understanding and to encourage the employee to express their thoughts and concerns. Repeat or paraphrase their statements to demonstrate that you are actively engaged, and to clarify any potential misunderstandings. This will create an open and collaborative environment, fostering trust and encouraging the employee to be more receptive to your feedback.

Finally, always be mindful of your tone and body language. Maintain a calm and composed demeanor, ensuring that your non-verbal cues align with your message. Avoid aggressive or confrontational language, as this can escalate the situation and hinder effective communication.

By using clear and concise language, you can navigate tough conversations with employees more effectively. Your ability to communicate clearly will foster understanding, build trust, and improve the overall relationship between you and your employees. Remember, difficult conversations are an opportunity for growth and improvement, and using clear and concise language is a valuable tool to help you achieve positive outcomes.

Choosing the Right Time and Place for Conversations

Within the domain of employee management, the need for challenging conversations is inevitable. These dialogues may delve into sensitive subjects like performance concerns, conflicts, or even termination. For employers, it is vital to approach these discussions with careful consideration, ensuring they take place at the opportune time and in a suitable setting. This section delves into the significance of selecting the right timing and environment for engaging in difficult dialogues with employees.

Timing is everything when it comes to having challenging conversations. Selecting the right moment ensures that both parties are mentally prepared, focused, and receptive to the message being conveyed. It is crucial to avoid discussing sensitive matters when either the employer or the employee is rushed or distracted. The ideal time is when both parties can allocate sufficient time and energy to engage in a meaningful conversation without interruptions or time constraints.

Additionally, the emotional state of the employee should be taken into account when determining the appropriate timing. If an

employee is already under stress or dealing with personal issues, it may not be the right time to address difficult matters. Waiting for a calmer moment when the employee is in a more receptive mindset can significantly enhance the chances of a positive outcome.

Equally important is the choice of location for these conversations. Selecting a private and neutral space is vital to ensure confidentiality and minimize distractions. This setting allows both the employer and the employee to feel comfortable and safe, fostering open and honest communication. It also helps to prevent potential disruptions or eavesdropping, which could further escalate tensions or compromise the integrity of the conversation.

Consideration should also be given to the physical arrangement of the space. Opting for a face-to-face seating arrangement, such as sitting across a table, promotes equality and encourages open dialogue. Avoiding physical barriers, like desks or walls, can help create a more collaborative and empathetic environment.

By carefully choosing the right time and place for difficult conversations with employees, employers can create a conducive atmosphere for constructive dialogue. This approach not only increases the chances of a successful outcome but also demonstrates respect and empathy towards the employee. Ultimately, navigating tough conversations with sensitivity and thoughtfulness can contribute to stronger employee relationships, improved performance, and a healthier work environment.

Non-Verbal Communication Cues and Body Language

In the realm of difficult dialogue, understanding non-verbal communication cues and body language is essential for employers to effectively navigate tough conversations with employees. Often, what is left unsaid or conveyed through non-verbal cues can have a profound impact on the outcome of these conversations.

Non-verbal communication cues encompass a wide range of expressions, gestures, and postures that convey emotions, attitudes, and intentions. Employers must pay close attention to these cues as they can reveal valuable insights into an employee's mindset and feelings during challenging discussions.

One crucial aspect of non-verbal communication is body language. How an employee positions their body, their facial expressions, and even their eye contact can provide significant clues about their level of engagement, comfort, or defensiveness. For example, crossed arms or averted eye contact may indicate defensiveness or discomfort, while leaning forward and maintaining eye contact may signify attentiveness and openness.

Understanding body language can help employers gauge the impact of their words and adjust their approach accordingly. By observing an employee's body language, employers can adapt their communication style to make the conversation more productive and conducive to a positive outcome. They can also identify signs of resistance or disengagement and address them proactively, ensuring that the concerns at hand are fully understood and addressed.

Additionally, non-verbal cues can help employers assess their own communication effectiveness. By paying attention to how employees react to their messages, employers can gauge whether their words are being received as intended. This self-awareness is crucial in fostering open and honest dialogue and ensuring that employers are effectively conveying their expectations and concerns.

To effectively utilize non-verbal communication cues and body language, employers must strive for empathy and active listening. By actively listening to both verbal and non-verbal cues, employers can create an environment where employees feel heard and understood. This empathetic approach helps build trust and rapport, enabling a more constructive conversation even in the face of difficult topics.

In summary, the proficiency to comprehend and interpret non-verbal communication cues and body language stands as a crucial skill for employers handling challenging discussions with their employees. By tuning into these cues and leveraging them as a compass, employers can tailor their communication style, tackle resistance, and promote open dialogue. Cultivating this skill set not only elevates the effectiveness of communication but also plays a pivotal role in achieving more productive and positive outcomes in difficult conversations with employees.

Chapter 5: Handling Difficult Reactions

Dealing with Defensive or Aggressive Behaviors

In the world of employment, it is inevitable that employers will have to engage in tough conversations with their employees from time to time. These conversations may arise due to various reasons such as performance issues, conflicts in the workplace, or addressing inappropriate behavior. However, one common challenge faced by employers in these conversations is dealing with defensive or aggressive behaviors exhibited by their employees.

Defensive behaviors can manifest in many ways, including denying responsibility, deflecting blame onto others, or becoming dismissive of feedback. On the other hand, aggressive behaviors can range from raised voices and verbal attacks to physical intimidation. Both types of behaviors can hinder productive dialogue and create a hostile work environment, making it crucial for employers to address them effectively.

The first step in handling defensive or aggressive behaviors is to remain calm and composed. It is essential to approach the conversation with a neutral mindset and avoid responding to aggression with aggression. Instead, focus on active listening and understanding the underlying concerns or frustrations that may be driving these behaviors. By acknowledging their feelings and concerns, you can help diffuse the defensiveness or aggression.

Another crucial aspect is setting clear boundaries. Make it explicitly known that such behaviors are not acceptable and will not be tolerated in the workplace. Reinforce the importance of respectful communication and emphasize that the purpose of the conversation is to find a solution or resolution. By setting these boundaries, you establish a framework for a constructive dialogue and encourage the employee to express their concerns in a more appropriate manner.

During the conversation, it is important to engage in open-ended questioning to encourage the employee to reflect on their behavior. This can help them gain self-awareness and understand the impact of their actions on themselves and others. Additionally, provide specific examples of their behavior and its consequences, highlighting how it goes against company values or policies. By doing so, you can help the employee recognize the need for change.

Finally, offer support and resources to help employees modify their behavior. This can include suggesting training programs, counseling, or mentorship opportunities that can assist them in developing better communication and conflict resolution skills. By providing these resources, employers demonstrate their commitment to helping employees grow and succeed.

Dealing with defensive or aggressive behaviors is undoubtedly challenging, but by approaching these conversations with empathy, setting clear boundaries, and offering support, employers can create a more inclusive and harmonious work environment. Remember, difficult conversations present an opportunity for growth and improvement, both for the employee and the organization as a whole.

Addressing Emotional Reactions and Resistance

As employers, one of the most challenging aspects of our role is having tough conversations with our employees. Whether it's addressing performance issues, discussing workplace conflicts, or delivering difficult feedback, these conversations can often elicit emotional reactions and resistance from the individuals involved. However, it is crucial for us to address these reactions effectively to ensure constructive dialogue and positive outcomes.

When confronted with emotional reactions, it is important to approach the situation with empathy and understanding. Recognize that emotions are a natural response to difficult conversations and validate the employee's feelings. Create a safe and supportive environment where they feel comfortable expressing their emotions without fear of judgment or retribution.

Active listening plays a vital role in addressing emotional reactions. Give the employee your undivided attention, maintain eye contact, and demonstrate genuine interest in their perspective. Reflect back on what they have shared to show that you understand and acknowledge their feelings. This validation can help to defuse tension and foster a more productive conversation.

It is also essential to manage your own emotions during these challenging discussions. Stay calm, composed, and professional, even if the employee becomes defensive or confrontational. Avoid becoming defensive yourself, as this can escalate the situation and hinder progress. Instead, focus on maintaining an open and non-judgmental stance, seeking to understand the underlying concerns and needs behind their emotional reactions.

Resistance is another common reaction during tough conversations. Employees may resist feedback, deny accountability, or become dismissive. To address resistance effectively, it is crucial to foster a collaborative and solution-oriented approach. Encourage the employee to share their perspective and actively involve them in problem-solving. This can help shift their mindset from defensiveness to a more constructive engagement with the conversation.

Furthermore, providing clear expectations and consequences can help manage resistance. Clearly communicate the desired outcomes of the conversation and the potential consequences of not addressing the issues at hand. This can motivate employees to take the conversation seriously and be more open to finding solutions.

Remember, addressing emotional reactions and resistance in tough conversations requires patience, empathy, and effective communication skills. By creating a safe space for dialogue, actively listening, managing your own emotions, and fostering collaboration, you can navigate these challenging conversations more successfully. Ultimately, these conversations present opportunities for growth and improvement, both for the employee and the organization as a whole.

Providing Constructive Feedback and Encouraging Accountability

In any workplace, difficult conversations with employees are bound to arise. Whether it's addressing performance issues, behavioral concerns, or conflicts within the team, employers must be equipped with the skills to navigate these tough conversations effectively. This subchapter aims to provide employers with actionable strategies for providing constructive feedback and encouraging accountability in their employees.

Constructive feedback is essential for employee growth and development. It involves providing honest and specific feedback that focuses on behaviors and outcomes rather than personal attacks. When delivering feedback, employers should aim to be specific, objective, and timely. It is crucial to prepare for the conversation by gathering relevant facts and examples to support your feedback. This will help ensure that your feedback is accurate and well-founded.

To encourage accountability, it is important to establish clear expectations and goals from the outset. Employers should clearly communicate what is expected of each employee and provide them with the necessary resources and support to meet those expectations. Regular check-ins and performance evaluations can help keep employees on track and provide opportunities for open dialogue about their progress.

When addressing performance issues or conflicts, employers should adopt a problem-solving approach. Rather than focusing solely on the negative aspects, it is beneficial to explore potential solutions together. Encourage employees to take ownership of their actions and work collaboratively to find ways to improve. This approach fosters a sense of accountability and empowers employees to take responsibility for their own growth and development.

During difficult conversations, it is essential to maintain an open and non-judgmental mindset. Active listening is key – allow employees to express their thoughts and concerns without interruption. By showing empathy and understanding, employers can create a safe and supportive environment that encourages honest communication.

Finally, it is important to follow up on the conversation with a plan of action. Summarize the key points discussed and document any agreed-upon action steps. Regularly revisit these action steps to ensure progress is being made and provide ongoing feedback and support.

To sum up, providing constructive feedback and encouraging accountability is a crucial aspect of effective employee management. By adopting these strategies, employers can create a positive work environment that fosters growth, development, and open communication.

Chapter 6: Resolving Conflict and Reaching Solutions

Identifying Common Ground and Shared Interests

Within the sphere of employee management, engaging in challenging conversations is unavoidable. For employers, it is imperative to navigate these discussions with finesse and empathy, ensuring that both parties feel acknowledged and understood. A pivotal strategy to accomplish this involves identifying common ground and shared interests.

When engaging in tough conversations with employees, it is natural for disagreements and conflicts to arise. However, it is essential to remember that beneath the surface, there are often shared interests and common goals that can bridge the gap between differing viewpoints. By identifying these commonalities, employers can establish a foundation of understanding and build a more productive dialogue.

The first step in identifying common ground is active listening. Take the time to truly hear your employees' concerns, opinions, and perspectives. By listening attentively, you not only validate their experiences but also gain valuable insights into their underlying motivations. This allows you to identify points of convergence and potential shared interests more effectively.

Another valuable approach is to seek out shared goals. While your employee's methods or ideas might differ from yours, the ultimate objective is often the same. By focusing on the common goal, you can steer the conversation away from personal differences and towards a collaborative problem-solving approach. This not only helps in finding a resolution but also builds trust and cooperation between you and your employees.

Additionally, recognizing shared values can also be a powerful tool in navigating tough conversations. Core values, such as respect, fairness, and open communication, are often shared by both parties. By emphasizing these shared values, you can create a sense of unity and reinforce the belief that everyone involved wants what is best for the company and its employees.

Identifying common ground and shared interests is not about compromising or abandoning your position as an employer. Instead, it is about finding commonalities that can serve as a starting point for meaningful dialogue and problem-solving. By doing so, you create an atmosphere of collaboration, where both parties feel valued and respected.

In conclusion, difficult conversations with employees can be challenging, but by identifying common ground and shared interests, employers can navigate these conversations more effectively. By actively listening, seeking shared goals, and recognizing shared values, employers can create a foundation of understanding and collaboration. Ultimately, this approach fosters a healthier work environment, improves employee satisfaction, and leads to more successful outcomes for both the company and its employees.

Exploring Different Perspectives and Generating Options

Within the domain of challenging discussions with employees, a paramount skill for employers to cultivate is the capacity to explore diverse perspectives and generate options. This section will delve into the significance of embracing various viewpoints and offer practical strategies for crafting creative solutions.

When engaging in difficult dialogues with employees, it is essential to recognize that there are often multiple perspectives at play. Each individual brings their own unique set of experiences, values, and beliefs to the table. By actively seeking out and considering these different perspectives, employers can gain a more comprehensive understanding of the situation and foster a more inclusive and collaborative work environment.

Exploring different perspectives involves creating a safe space for open and honest communication. Employers should encourage employees to share their thoughts, concerns, and ideas without fear of judgment or reprisal. By actively listening and validating their perspectives, employers can build trust and establish a foundation for productive dialogue.

To generate options, employers should foster a culture of creativity and innovation. Encourage employees to think outside the box and explore unconventional solutions. Brainstorming sessions and team discussions can be excellent platforms for generating a wide range of options. Employers should emphasize the importance of respecting all ideas and refrain from prematurely judging or dismissing suggestions.

Another effective strategy for generating options is to encourage employees to consider different scenarios and potential outcomes. This helps broaden the range of possibilities and allows for a more thorough exploration of potential solutions. By encouraging employees to analyze the pros and cons of each option, employers can facilitate a comprehensive decision-making process.

It is important for employers to remember that generating options does not mean finding a one-size-fits-all solution. Each employee may have different needs and preferences, and it is crucial to tailor the conversation accordingly. Employers should be flexible and open to finding creative compromises that meet the interests of all parties involved.

In summary, exploring different perspectives and generating options is a crucial aspect of navigating tough conversations with employees. By actively seeking out diverse viewpoints and fostering a culture of creativity and innovation, employers can facilitate constructive dialogue and find effective solutions. Embracing this approach will not only improve communication and teamwork but also contribute to a more inclusive and harmonious work environment.

Negotiating and Finding Win-Win Solutions

In the realm of managing employees, difficult conversations are an inevitable part of the job. Addressing issues such as performance concerns, conflicts, or behavioral problems may seem daunting, but they are essential for maintaining a healthy work environment. The key to successfully navigating these tough conversations lies in negotiating and finding win-win solutions that benefit both the employer and the employees involved.

Negotiation is a skill that every employer should develop to effectively handle challenging discussions with their employees. It requires a delicate balance between assertiveness and empathy, ensuring that both parties feel heard and understood. Approaching these conversations with a win-win mindset fosters collaboration and promotes a positive outcome for everyone involved.

First and foremost, it is crucial to create an environment of trust and open communication. Employees should feel comfortable expressing their concerns and ideas without fear of retribution. Active listening is a fundamental aspect of this process, allowing employers to gain a deeper understanding of the employees' perspectives and concerns. By acknowledging their viewpoints, employers can build rapport and establish a foundation for finding mutually beneficial solutions.

When negotiating, it is essential to focus on interests rather than positions. Understanding the underlying needs and motivations of both parties allows for creative problem-solving. By exploring various alternatives, employers can discover solutions that meet the needs of the organization while also addressing the employees' concerns. This approach requires flexibility and a willingness to explore unconventional options, often leading to innovative outcomes that surpass initial expectations.

A win-win solution emphasizes collaboration and compromise. It involves finding common ground and identifying shared goals that align with both the employer's and employees' interests. By involving employees in the decision-making process, employers empower them and foster a sense of ownership and commitment. This not only enhances job satisfaction but also promotes a positive work culture built on trust and respect.

Negotiating and finding win-win solutions may not always be easy, but it is crucial for employers when handling tough conversations with employees. By cultivating a mindset of collaboration and empathy, employers can create an environment that encourages open dialogue and problem-solving. This subchapter will provide employers with valuable insights, strategies, and practical tips to master the art of negotiation and find win-win solutions that lead to positive outcomes for all parties involved.

Chapter 7: Follow-Up and Continuous Improvement

Documenting Conversations and Agreements

In the context of navigating difficult conversations with employees, an often understated but pivotal element is the necessity of documenting these discussions and any resulting agreements. Proper documentation is not only a legal safeguard but also a cornerstone for maintaining clarity, accountability, and consistency in the workplace. This subsection will scrutinize the critical reasons why documenting conversations and agreements is indispensable, providing practical insights into how employers can seamlessly integrate this practice.

First and foremost, documentation serves as a legal protection for employers. In the event of a dispute or legal action, having a written record of conversations and agreements can be invaluable. It provides evidence of what was discussed, agreed upon, and any subsequent actions taken. By documenting these interactions, employers can minimize the risk of misunderstandings, false claims, or differing recollections.

Additionally, proper documentation fosters clarity and accountability. Employees may have varying interpretations of a conversation or agreement, which can lead to confusion and conflicts down the line. By documenting these exchanges, both parties have a clear reference point to ensure they are on the same page. This clarity promotes accountability, as employees are more likely to adhere to agreements when they are explicitly spelled out in writing.

Consistency is another crucial benefit of documenting conversations and agreements. When tough conversations occur, it is essential to handle them consistently across the board. By documenting these interactions, employers can ensure that similar situations are approached in a uniform manner. This consistency is vital for maintaining fairness and avoiding potential claims of favoritism or discrimination.

To effectively implement documentation practices, employers should follow a few key tips. Firstly, document conversations promptly while the details are fresh in everyone's minds. Be thorough and include relevant details such as date, time, location, participants, and a summary of the conversation. Use objective language and avoid personal opinions or biases. Finally, ensure that both parties review and sign the documentation to acknowledge their agreement and understanding.

In conclusion, documenting conversations and agreements is a critical component of navigating tough conversations with employees. It provides legal protection, fosters clarity and accountability, and promotes consistency in the workplace. By implementing proper documentation practices, employers can create a transparent and fair environment, reducing the risk of misunderstandings and conflicts. Remember, when it comes to tough conversations, "if it's not documented, it didn't happen."

Monitoring Progress and Providing Support

Within the arena of employee management, engaging in challenging conversations is unavoidable. Be it addressing performance concerns, conflicts, or navigating through difficult situations, employers frequently encounter dialogues that demand finesse. These discussions can be uncomfortable, emotionally charged, and possess the potential to strain workplace relationships. Nevertheless, by implementing effective strategies to monitor progress and offer support, employers can navigate these tough conversations with tact and empathy, ultimately fostering growth and development within their teams.

Monitoring progress is an essential aspect of managing employees and ensuring their success. Regularly assessing performance allows employers to identify areas of improvement and provide timely feedback. By setting clear expectations and establishing measurable goals, employers can track progress and address any deviations promptly. Regular check-ins and performance reviews provide opportunities to discuss achievements, challenges, and future plans, ensuring alignment between employee and organizational objectives. This continuous monitoring not only helps in identifying and resolving issues promptly but also encourages a proactive approach to problem-solving.

However, monitoring progress alone is not enough. Providing adequate support is equally crucial to help employees overcome challenges and improve performance. When engaging in tough conversations, employers should approach them with empathy, actively listening to their employees' concerns and perspectives. By acknowledging their feelings and validating their experiences, employers create a safe and supportive environment for dialogue. Additionally, offering resources, training, and mentorship programs can empower employees to enhance their skills and address any performance gaps effectively.

During tough conversations, it is essential for employers to practice effective communication techniques. This includes being clear, concise, and specific in their feedback. Employers should focus on behavior and outcomes rather than personal attacks. Constructive criticism should be delivered in a respectful manner, ensuring that the employee feels heard and understood. Offering alternative perspectives and brainstorming solutions together can also foster a sense of collaboration and mutual understanding.

Ultimately, monitoring progress and providing support in difficult dialogues with employees is a delicate balance between holding employees accountable for their performance and creating a supportive environment for growth. By implementing these strategies, employers can navigate tough conversations with empathy, open-mindedness, and professionalism, leading to a more productive and harmonious workplace.

Learning from Each Conversation and Improving Communication Skills

Effective communication is an essential skill for employers, especially when it comes to navigating tough conversations with employees. These difficult dialogues can arise from various situations, such as addressing performance issues, delivering feedback, or dealing with conflicts in the workplace. However, rather than avoiding or dreading these conversations, employers should view them as learning opportunities that can help improve their communication skills.

One of the key aspects of learning from each conversation is active listening. It is crucial to listen attentively to the concerns, perspectives, and emotions of employees during these tough conversations. By truly understanding their viewpoints, employers can gain valuable insights into the underlying issues and work towards finding mutually beneficial solutions. Additionally, active listening demonstrates respect and empathy, which can help build trust and rapport with employees.

Furthermore, employers should reflect on their own communication style and identify areas for improvement. While it is easy to focus solely on the employee's behavior or performance, self-reflection allows employers to assess how their communication approach may have contributed to the difficulty of the conversation. This self-awareness can lead to adjustments in communication techniques, such as using more inclusive language, providing clearer instructions, or utilizing active questioning to encourage dialogue.

Another valuable strategy for improving communication skills is seeking feedback from employees. After each tough conversation, employers can ask for feedback on how they handled the conversation and what could have been done differently. This feedback loop not only shows a commitment to continuous improvement but also provides valuable insights into employees' perceptions and expectations. It allows employers to adapt their communication style and approach to better meet the needs of their team members.

In addition to individual learning, employers can promote a culture of open communication within their organization. By encouraging employees to share their thoughts and concerns, employers create an environment where tough conversations become more manageable. Regular team meetings, feedback sessions, and anonymous suggestion boxes are all effective ways to foster open communication and create a safe space for dialogue.

To conclude, difficult dialogues with employees should be seen as opportunities for growth and improvement in communication skills. Active listening, self-reflection, seeking feedback, and promoting open communication are all essential elements in this process. By continuously learning from each conversation, employers can enhance their communication skills, build stronger relationships with employees, and create a more harmonious and productive work environment.

Chapter 8: Special Considerations in Difficult Conversations

Addressing Performance Issues and Corrective Actions

In any organization, employers may occasionally be faced with the daunting task of addressing performance issues and implementing corrective actions with their employees. These tough conversations can be challenging, but they are vital for maintaining a productive and harmonious work environment. In this subchapter, we will explore effective strategies to navigate such difficult dialogues with employees.

When addressing performance issues, it is crucial to approach the conversation with empathy and understanding. Recognize that employees may be facing personal challenges or lack the necessary resources to excel in their roles. By adopting a compassionate mindset, employers can create an atmosphere that encourages open communication and mutual growth.

To begin, it is important to establish clear expectations and goals for employees. By setting realistic targets and providing regular feedback, employers can help employees understand where they stand and what is expected of them. Open lines of communication are crucial in ensuring that employees feel comfortable discussing any challenges they face.

When discussing performance issues, it is essential to focus on the behavior or outcomes rather than criticizing the individual. A constructive approach involves discussing specific incidents or situations, providing examples, and emphasizing the impact of their actions on the team or the organization. This allows employees to reflect on their performance and understand the need for improvement without feeling attacked.

During these conversations, employers should actively listen to employees' concerns and perspectives. Encourage them to share their side of the story and actively seek solutions together. By involving employees in problem-solving, employers can foster a sense of ownership and accountability, making it more likely that they will be committed to implementing corrective actions.

Corrective actions should be tailored to the individual and the specific performance issue. This could involve additional training, coaching, or mentoring, depending on the employee's needs. Regular check-ins and follow-ups are crucial to monitor progress and provide ongoing support.

It is also important to document these conversations and any agreed-upon actions. This documentation serves as a reference point for future discussions and can provide clarity in case of further performance issues.

Addressing performance issues and implementing corrective actions can be uncomfortable, but it is a necessary part of being an employer. By employing compassionate and constructive strategies, employers can navigate these difficult conversations with empathy, leading to improved performance, employee growth, and a more harmonious work environment.

Navigating Personal Issues and Confidentiality

Difficult Dialogue: Navigating Tough Conversations with Employees

Within the context of challenging discussions with employees, it is imperative for employers to tackle personal issues while upholding confidentiality. Personal matters can exert a considerable influence on an employee's performance and well-being, necessitating employers to approach these conversations with empathy, understanding, and professionalism.

Confidentiality is the cornerstone of trust between employers and employees. Employees need to feel comfortable sharing personal issues without fear of judgment or repercussions. By establishing a culture of confidentiality, employers can create a safe space for employees to open up about their personal struggles. This allows employers to better understand the underlying factors affecting an employee's performance and devise appropriate solutions.

When engaging in tough conversations related to personal issues, it is important to approach the situation with sensitivity. Begin by acknowledging the employee's feelings and letting them know that their personal well-being is a priority. Assure them that the conversation will remain confidential unless there are legal or safety concerns. By demonstrating empathy and understanding, employers can foster a supportive environment where employees feel valued and cared for.

Respecting confidentiality means that employers must exercise discretion when sharing information about an employee's personal issues with others in the workplace. It is essential to communicate the importance of maintaining confidentiality to all team members involved in the conversation. Remind them that breaching confidentiality not only undermines trust but can also have legal implications.

In some cases, personal issues may require additional support beyond what an employer can provide. In such situations, it is important to be aware of available resources and refer employees to appropriate professionals, such as therapists, counselors, or human resources specialists. By connecting employees with the necessary support systems, employers can further demonstrate their commitment to their employees' well-being.

It is crucial for employers to remember that personal issues can impact an employee's professional life and vice versa. By addressing personal issues in a confidential and supportive manner, employers can help employees navigate through difficult times while fostering a positive work environment.

To sum up, navigating personal issues and maintaining confidentiality is an integral part of engaging in tough conversations with employees. By establishing a culture of confidentiality, demonstrating empathy, and referring employees to appropriate resources, employers can effectively address personal issues while promoting a supportive work environment. Ultimately, prioritizing personal well-being contributes to employee satisfaction, productivity, and overall organizational success.

Handling Difficult Conversations in a Remote Work Environment

In today's ever-evolving work landscape, the concept of remote work has become increasingly common. With the rise of virtual teams, employers are facing new challenges when it comes to addressing sensitive topics and having difficult conversations with their employees. In this subchapter, we will explore effective strategies for handling tough conversations in a remote work environment.

1. Establish Clear Communication Channels: In a remote work environment, communication becomes even more crucial. Ensure that you have established clear channels for communication, such as video conferences, email, or instant messaging platforms. This will provide a reliable means for addressing difficult discussions with your employees.

2. Prepare in Advance: Before engaging in a difficult conversation, it is essential to prepare adequately. Clearly define the purpose of the discussion, identify the key points you want to address, and anticipate possible reactions or concerns from your employee. This preparation will allow you to approach the conversation with confidence and empathy.

3. Choose the Right Time and Place: Just as you would in a face-to-face setting, it is important to choose an appropriate time and place for the conversation. Ensure that both you and your employee have enough time to fully engage in the discussion without distractions. Scheduling a virtual meeting and giving advance notice will help set the right tone for the conversation.

4. Practice Active Listening: Remote conversations can sometimes be hindered by technological limitations or distractions. As an employer, it is crucial to practice active listening during tough conversations. Give your employee your undivided attention, ask clarifying questions, and acknowledge their feelings and concerns. This will create a safe space for open dialogue and understanding.

5. Use Visual Cues: In a remote work environment, non-verbal communication cues may be limited. However, utilizing visual cues can help convey empathy and understanding. Maintain eye contact, use facial expressions, and nod affirmatively to demonstrate your engagement and support.

6. Follow Up: After the conversation, follow up with your employee to ensure that they feel heard and supported. Providing additional resources or suggesting next steps can help them navigate the situation and address any concerns that may have arisen during the conversation.

In summary, handling difficult conversations in a remote work environment requires adaptability and effective communication strategies. By establishing clear channels, preparing in advance, choosing the right time and place, practicing active listening, utilizing visual cues, and following up, employers can successfully navigate tough conversations with their remote employees.

Chapter 9: Building a Culture of Open Communication

Creating an Environment that Encourages Dialogue

In today's diverse and dynamic workplace, employers often find themselves confronted with tough conversations with employees. These difficult dialogues can range from addressing performance issues to discussing sensitive topics such as workplace harassment or personal conflicts. However, it is crucial for employers to create an environment that encourages dialogue in order to effectively navigate these tough conversations and foster a healthy and productive workplace.

The first step in creating an environment that encourages dialogue is to establish an open-door policy. Employers should make it clear to their employees that they are approachable and willing to listen to any concerns or issues they may have. This can be done through regular communication channels such as team meetings, one-on-one sessions, or even anonymous suggestion boxes. By creating an atmosphere of trust and accessibility, employees will feel more comfortable sharing their thoughts and engaging in dialogue.

Another important aspect of fostering dialogue is to actively listen to employees. Employers should make a conscious effort to hear and understand what their employees are saying, without interrupting or passing judgment. Active listening involves paying attention to both verbal and non-verbal cues, asking clarifying questions, and summarizing the main points raised by the employee. This demonstrates to employees that their opinions matter and encourages them to express their thoughts more freely.

Furthermore, employers should create opportunities for dialogue and collaboration among employees. This can be done through team-building activities, group projects, or cross-functional teams. By encouraging employees to work together and exchange ideas, employers foster a culture of open communication and collaboration. This not only helps in diffusing potential conflicts but also promotes a more inclusive and innovative work environment.

Additionally, employers should provide training and resources to their employees on effective communication and conflict resolution. This can include workshops, seminars, or access to online resources that teach employees how to engage in constructive dialogue, manage emotions, and resolve conflicts in a respectful manner. Equipping employees with these skills not only enhances their ability to engage in tough conversations but also empowers them to handle difficult situations more effectively.

Lastly, creating an environment that encourages dialogue is essential for employers when navigating tough conversations with employees. By establishing an open-door policy, actively listening, promoting collaboration, and providing training on effective communication, employers can foster a workplace where tough conversations are approached with respect and understanding. This not only leads to better resolutions but also contributes to a more positive and productive work environment overall.

Training and Developing Managers in Difficult Conversation Skills

Effective communication is essential in the workplace, and this is especially true when it comes to difficult conversations with employees. These conversations can arise in various situations, such as addressing poor performance, discussing behavioral issues, or delivering negative feedback. To ensure these conversations are handled professionally and productively, it is crucial for employers to train and develop their managers in difficult conversation skills.

In this subchapter, we will focus on the importance of training and

developing managers in difficult conversation skills and provide practical tips for achieving success.

The first step in training managers in difficult conversation skills is to create awareness of the importance of these skills. Employers must emphasize the impact that effective communication can have on employee morale, productivity, and overall success. By understanding the significance of these conversations, managers will be motivated to enhance their skills and approach them with confidence.

Next, employers should provide managers with the necessary tools and resources to develop their communication skills. This can include workshops, seminars, or online courses that specifically address difficult conversation techniques. Practical exercises and role-playing scenarios can also be incorporated to allow managers to practice their skills in a safe and supportive environment.

Additionally, it is crucial to provide ongoing support and feedback to managers as they navigate difficult conversations. Employers should establish a culture of open communication, where managers feel comfortable seeking guidance and sharing their experiences. Regular check-ins and coaching sessions can help managers refine their skills and address any challenges they may encounter.

Furthermore, employers should encourage a growth mindset among managers regarding difficult conversations. It is essential to view these conversations as opportunities for growth and development rather than merely difficult tasks to be completed. By fostering this mindset, managers will approach these conversations with a willingness to learn and adapt their communication style to best suit the needs of their employees.

In a nutshell, effective communication is at the core of successful difficult conversations with employees. By training and developing managers in difficult conversation skills, employers can ensure that these conversations are handled professionally and productively. Difficult Dialogue: Navigating Tough Conversations with Employees serves as a valuable resource to help employers navigate these challenging conversations and foster a positive and productive work environment.

Fostering Employee Feedback and Encouraging Peer Conversations

In the world of business, effective communication is key to building strong relationships, nurturing a positive work environment, and achieving organizational success. However, engaging in tough conversations with employees can be a daunting task for any employer. These difficult dialogues may arise due to performance issues, conflicts, or other sensitive matters. Nevertheless, it is crucial for employers to tackle these conversations head-on in order to foster growth, development, and harmony within the workplace.

One powerful tool that employers can utilize to navigate these tough conversations is the promotion of employee feedback.

Encouraging open and honest feedback allows employees to share their thoughts, concerns, and suggestions regarding their work environment, processes, and policies. By creating a safe space for feedback, employers are not only empowering their employees but also gaining valuable insights that can lead to positive change. This approach can help identify potential issues before they escalate, as well as enhance overall employee satisfaction and engagement.

To foster employee feedback, it is important for employers to establish channels for communication. Whether it is through regular team meetings, suggestion boxes, or designated feedback sessions, employers must create platforms that encourage employees to express their opinions and concerns. Additionally, it is crucial for employers to actively listen to feedback and take appropriate actions based on the information received. This demonstrates a commitment to employee well-being and reinforces a culture of trust and transparency.

In addition to fostering employee feedback, encouraging peer conversations can also be highly beneficial. Peer conversations provide employees with the opportunity to share ideas, learn from one another, and support each other through challenges. Employers can facilitate peer conversations by implementing collaborative projects, team-building activities, or mentorship programs. These initiatives not only promote teamwork and collaboration but also foster a sense of camaraderie among employees.

By encouraging peer conversations, employers create an environment where employees feel comfortable seeking guidance from their colleagues and resolving conflicts in a constructive manner. This can significantly reduce the burden on employers when it comes to managing difficult conversations directly. Moreover, peer conversations contribute to a continuous learning culture, where employees can develop their skills, share best practices, and ultimately contribute to the growth of the organization.

To wrap up, fostering employee feedback and encouraging peer conversations are essential strategies for employers when navigating tough conversations with employees. By actively seeking and listening to feedback, employers gain valuable insights that can lead to positive change. Additionally, promoting peer conversations empowers employees to support one another, resolve conflicts, and continuously learn and grow. By implementing these strategies, employers can create a harmonious work environment that fosters open communication, employee engagement, and long-term success.

Chapter 10: Case Studies and Examples

Difficult Dialogue Scenario 1: Addressing Attendance Issues

Attendance issues can be a common problem that employers face when managing their employees. Whether it's chronic lateness, frequent absences, or unexplained disappearances during work hours, addressing attendance concerns can be a challenging and uncomfortable task. However, it is essential for employers to navigate these tough conversations with employees in order to maintain a productive and efficient workplace.

When addressing attendance issues, it is crucial for employers to approach the conversation with empathy and understanding. It is essential to remember that employees may be facing personal or health-related challenges that affect their attendance. By starting the conversation with an open mind and a willingness to listen, employers can establish a more conducive environment for productive dialogue.

Begin the conversation by expressing appreciation for the employee's work and contributions to the company. This helps to create a positive tone and ensures that the employee feels valued despite the attendance concerns. Next, discuss the specific instances or patterns of attendance problems, providing concrete examples to illustrate the issue. This allows the employee to understand the extent of the problem and its impact on their job performance and team dynamics.

During the conversation, it is important to inquire about any potential underlying issues that may be causing the attendance problems. This could include personal or family matters, health issues, or even dissatisfaction with their current role or work environment. By demonstrating empathy and understanding, employers can create a safe space for employees to openly share their concerns and challenges.

Once the underlying issues are identified, work together with the employee to develop a plan of action. This may involve setting clear attendance expectations, offering flexible scheduling options, or providing necessary resources and support. Collaborative problem-solving not only empowers the employee to take ownership of their attendance issues but also strengthens the employer-employee relationship.

Conclude the conversation by reiterating the importance of attendance and its impact on the employee's career growth and the overall success of the company. Offer ongoing support and regular check-ins to monitor progress and address any further concerns or challenges that may arise.

Navigating tough conversations about attendance issues requires employers to balance empathy, understanding, and firmness. By approaching these dialogues with a solution-oriented mindset, employers can foster a culture of open communication and accountability, leading to improved attendance and a more harmonious work environment.

Difficult Dialogue Scenario 2: Dealing with Performance Concerns

Addressed to Employers in the Niche of Tough Conversations with Employees

Introduction:

As an employer, one of the most challenging aspects of managing a team is addressing performance concerns with employees. These difficult conversations can be uncomfortable and sensitive, but they are necessary for the growth and success of both the individual and the organization. This subchapter aims to provide guidance on how to navigate such scenarios effectively.

Understanding the Importance of Performance Conversations:

Performance concerns left unaddressed can lead to a decline in productivity, a negative impact on team morale, and ultimately, unsatisfactory results. It is crucial to approach these conversations with empathy, clarity, and a focus on finding solutions that benefit both the employee and the company.

Preparing for the Conversation:

Before engaging in a performance conversation, it is essential to gather all the relevant facts and evidence to support your concerns. This can include performance metrics, examples of specific incidents, and feedback from colleagues or clients. Additionally, consider the employee's perspective and any underlying factors that may be contributing to their performance issues.

Setting the Tone:

Approach the conversation with a mindset of constructive feedback and improvement rather than criticism. Create a safe and non-confrontational environment by choosing a private and neutral location for the discussion. Begin the conversation by acknowledging the employee's strengths and contributions, emphasizing that the purpose of the conversation is to help them reach their full potential.

Active Listening and Open Communication:

During the dialogue, practice active listening to gain a deeper understanding of the employee's perspective. Encourage them to share their thoughts, concerns, and ideas for improvement. Maintain open and honest communication, fostering a two-way dialogue that allows for collaboration and problem-solving.

Setting Clear Expectations and Goals:

To ensure the conversation leads to positive change, provide specific examples of where the employee's performance falls short and how it impacts the team and the organization. Collaboratively establish clear expectations and mutually agreed-upon goals for improvement. Offer support, resources, and training opportunities that will enable the employee to succeed.

Follow-up and Continued Support:

Conclude the conversation by summarizing the key points discussed and outlining a plan of action moving forward. Schedule regular check-ins to monitor progress, provide guidance and support, and celebrate achievements. Remember that ongoing feedback and recognition are vital for maintaining employee motivation and growth.

Conclusion:

Difficult conversations surrounding performance concerns are a necessary part of being an employer. By approaching these dialogues with empathy, preparation, and open communication, employers can create an environment that fosters growth, accountability, and success for both the individual employee and the organization as a whole. Remember, these conversations are an opportunity for improvement and can lead to positive outcomes when handled with care and respect.

Difficult Dialogue Scenario 3: Resolving Interpersonal Conflict

In the domain of difficult discussions with employees, navigating one of the most intricate scenarios involves resolving interpersonal conflicts. As an employer, your pivotal role in effectively addressing and resolving these conflicts is crucial, given their potential impact on workplace morale, productivity, and overall team dynamics.

When faced with an interpersonal conflict, it's important to approach the situation with empathy, fairness, and a commitment to finding a resolution that benefits all parties involved. Here are some strategies to help you navigate and resolve such conflicts:

1. Encourage open communication: Create a safe and non-judgmental space where employees can express their concerns and perspectives. Encourage active listening and ensure that both parties have an opportunity to speak without interruption. This will help foster understanding and empathy between the conflicting parties.

2. Identify the underlying issues: Interpersonal conflicts often arise from deeper underlying issues, such as miscommunication, differences in values or work styles, or unresolved past conflicts. Take the time to uncover these root causes to address the conflict at its core rather than simply dealing with the surface-level symptoms.

3. Facilitate a constructive dialogue: Guide the conversation towards constructive problem-solving rather than dwelling on blame or personal attacks. Encourage the conflicting parties to focus on finding common ground and exploring potential solutions together. This will help shift the dynamic from a confrontational one to a collaborative one.

4. Mediate if necessary: If the conflict persists or escalates, consider bringing in a neutral third party to mediate the conversation. A trained mediator can help facilitate a more productive dialogue and assist in finding a mutually satisfactory resolution. Mediation can be especially helpful when the conflict involves power imbalances or deeply ingrained issues.

5. Follow up and provide support: After the conflict has been resolved, follow up with the individuals involved to ensure that the resolution is being implemented effectively. Provide ongoing support and guidance to prevent the conflict from reemerging or escalating. Consider implementing conflict resolution training or workshops to equip employees with the necessary skills to handle conflicts in the future.

Resolving interpersonal conflicts is a challenging yet essential aspect of managing a productive and harmonious work environment. By approaching these conversations with empathy, open communication, and a commitment to finding common ground, you can navigate tough interpersonal conflicts and foster a culture of collaboration and understanding within your organization.

In summary: Embracing Difficult Conversations for Growth and Success

In the fast-paced and ever-changing world of business, employers often find themselves faced with the challenge of navigating tough conversations with their employees. These difficult dialogues can range from addressing performance issues to discussing sensitive topics such as diversity and inclusion. However, it is crucial for employers to embrace these conversations as opportunities for growth and success, both for themselves and their employees.

One of the key reasons why embracing difficult conversations is essential is that it fosters a culture of open communication within the workplace. By creating an environment where employees feel comfortable discussing challenging topics, employers can address issues before they escalate and negatively impact the overall productivity and morale of the team. This open dialogue also encourages employees to share their perspectives and ideas, leading to innovation and improved problem-solving.

Furthermore, difficult conversations provide an opportunity for personal and professional growth. When employers engage in these discussions, they demonstrate their commitment to the development of their employees. By providing constructive feedback and guidance, employers can help their employees identify areas for improvement and offer resources for enhancing their skills. This investment in their employees' growth not only strengthens the organization but also builds trust and loyalty.

Embracing difficult conversations also allows employers to address diversity and inclusion within the workplace. By openly discussing these topics, employers can create a safe space for employees to share their experiences and concerns. This dialogue enables employers to understand and address any biases or inequalities that may exist, fostering a more inclusive and equitable work environment.

It is important for employers to approach difficult conversations with empathy and understanding. Actively listening to employees' perspectives and concerns, providing support, and showing appreciation for their contributions are all essential components of a successful dialogue. Employers should also be open to feedback and willing to adapt their approach as needed.

To draw the discussion to a close, embracing difficult conversations is crucial for employers seeking growth and success in their organizations. By fostering open communication, encouraging personal and professional growth, and addressing diversity and inclusion, employers can cultivate a culture of trust, innovation, and collaboration. These tough conversations may be challenging, but they are also opportunities for learning and improvement. By embracing them, employers can create a more resilient and successful workplace for both themselves and their employees.

Difficult Dialogue: Navigating Tough Conversations with Employees

www.ingramcontent.com/pod-product-compliance
Lightning Source LLC
Chambersburg PA
CBHW070117010626
45794CB00013B/2569